Introduction

There is no such thing as an ordinary rock. Every rock has been on an amazing, often violent, journey from deep inside the Earth to the surface and back to the depths again. A journey that took millions, even billions of years, and along the way turned carbon to diamond, limestone to marble and organisms to coal. Rocks provide us with minerals, metals, fuels, building materials, gems and so much more. From now on, you will never take a rock for granted ever again.

Contents

Read on to discover Earth's deepest and most colourful secrets...

A world of rocks

Rocks tell the **history** of the Earth and rocks will provide the materials to build Earth's future and our **future**. The planet's outer **layers** are made of rock and throughout history humankind has used this resource. In the **Stone Age**, rocks provided shelter and **weapons** and even the pigments for cave paintings. The Copper, Bronze and **Iron Ages** are so named because that is when humans learned to extract **minerals** in rocks to make metal **tools**, weapons, utensils and ornamental objects. Even in the **Space Age**, rocks and minerals provide essential resources.

Facts and figures

Metals in rocks

These metals are found in rocks in the Earth's crust. Rocks that contain metals are called ores.

Metal: Gold
Ore: Native gold
This soft metal is used in computers, jewellery and even spacesuit visors!

Metal: Silver
Ore: Acanthite
Once used to make coins, silver is found in jewellery, solar panels, and medical dressings.

Metal: Platinum
Ore: Sperrylite
This grey-white metal, often valued above gold, is used in jewellery and catalytic converters for vehicles.

Metal: Uranium
Ore: Uraninite
This is used in nuclear fission, which has applications in power generation, weapons and medicine.

The Earth is at least 4.4 billion years old!

The Danxia Landform in China has multi-coloured ridges made from red sandstone and mineral deposits

What's petrology?

Petrology is the study of the origin and composition of rocks. It is a branch of geology, which is the study of Earth's structure.

Hard and soft rocks

The minerals in a rock will cause it to be 'hard' or 'soft' and resistant or not to water. Hard rocks are often metamorphic or igneous, while soft rocks are usually sedimentary.

Did you know?

The oldest rocks on Earth are meteorites that formed in space before crashing on Earth. The Hoba Meteorite in Namibia, Africa, is the largest meteorite so far discovered.

Visu ers

C s

an s

Published in 2019 by Franklin Watts,
Carmelite House, 50 Victoria Embankment
London, EC4Y 0DZ, United Kingdom

Created and produced by:
Green Android Ltd
49 Beaumont Court
Upper Clapton Road
London E5 8BG
United Kingdom

MIX
Paper from responsible sources
FSC www.fsc.org
FSC® C104723

ISBN 978-1-4451-6816-6

Printed and bound in Dongguan, China, June 2019

Franklin Watts is a division of Hachette Children's Books
An Hachette UK company
www.hachette.co.uk

Image credits: (t) top, (m) middle, (b) bottom, (r) right, (l) left, (FF) Fact file.
Corbis – p26 (main) POOL/Reuters.

Flickr – FC (2nd) Stan Celestian. BC (3rd) Brian Penfold. **p10** (bl) photoa99. **p12** (bl) Andrew Porter. **p16** (bl) Patty. **p17** (t) Pauline and John Grimshaw. **p19** FF (b) Jose Eliécer Garcia Arango. **p27** (ml) Steven Zucker, (mr) Victoria and Albert Museum, London, IS.3&A-1982. **p28** (bl) Metal Chris. **p30** (bl) Stan Celestian. **p31** (m) John Kittelsrud.

Getty – p16 (main) Tim Gerard Barker. **p21** (b) Carsten Peter/Speleoresearch and Films. **p27** FF (t) Harry Taylor. **p31** (b) Sam Abell.

iStock – BC (4th), **p29** (t) Robert Kacpura.

p21 (m) J W Valley, University of Wisconsin-Madison.

Shutterstock – FC (main) LVV, (1st) Tomaz Kunst, (3rd) Lucky-photographer, (4th) Albert Russ. Spine Denis Vrublevski. BC (1st) Ammit Jack, (2nd) Vitya Serendipity. **p1** Wollertz. **p2-3** Tatsiana Selivanava. **p4** (main) Rat007, (bl) Jakub Houdek. **p5** (t) www.sandatlas.org, (m) Imfoto, (b) Sergey Lavrentev; FF Tyler Boyes. **p6** (main) Wollertz, (bl) robertloamphoto. **p7** (t) Pyty, (m) Francesco R. Iacomino, (b) Chris Warham; FF (t) LSkywalker, (b, Earth) Ismagilov. **p8** (main) Wead, (bl) Vladislav. **p9** (t) Digital Globe/Scapeware3D, (m) Fexel, (b) Paul Nash; FF (t) MarcelClemens, (m) www.sandatlas.org, (b) Tyler Boyes. **p10** (main) filmlandscape. **p11** (t) sigur, (m) www.sandatlas.org, (b) Les Palenik; FF (t, b) Tyler Boyes, (m) Sementer. **p12** (main) Richard Bowden. **p13** (t) VLADJ55, (m) Michael Steden, (b) www.sandatlas.org. **p14** (main) 501room, (bl) Bernd Leitner Fotodesign. **p15** (t) piotrwzk, (m) Michal Ninger, (b) Ansis Klucis. **p17** (t) Tsuguliev, (m) happystock, (b) Francesco R. Iacomino; FF (m) Patricia Hofmeester, (b) mikeledray. **p18** (main) bumihills, (bl) Artesia Wells. **p19** (tl) Mcincredible, (tm, tr) Geroge W. Bailey, (m) Hung Chung Chih, (b) Alexander Tihonov; FF (t) jl661227, (m) Dmitry Chulor. **p20** (main) Robert D Pinna, (bl) Vadim Sadovski. **p21** (tl) Vita Serendipity, (tr) AG Guesta. **p22** (main) Albert Russ, (bl) Stocksnapper. **p23** (t) Albert Russ, (m) jmboix, (bl) Nadezda Bottaca, (br) J. Palys; FF (t) Sementer, (mb) Imfoto. **p24** (main) Nastya22, (bl) Imfoto. **p25** (t) Stefano Cavoretto, (ml, mr, b) Albert Russ; FF (t) Whiteaster, (m) ET1972, (b) Marcel Clemens. **p26** (bl) J. Palys. **p27** (tr) Imfoto, (tl) Boykung, (bl) Ivan Smuk, (br) Miriam Doerr; FF (m) Texturis, (b) Hayati Kayhan. **p28** (main) Denis Vrubleuski. **p29** (m) Alice Nerr, (b) botazsotti. **p30** (main) Dusit. **p31** (t) Ivonne Wierink. **p32** Russell Shively.

Quartzite is a hard metamorphic rock

Sunstone is an orange coloured feldspar

What is a rock...

A rock is naturally formed from a mixture of one or more minerals that have clumped together into a solid lump. Quartzite rock consists of one mineral (quartz) while granite is a mixture of 11 minerals. Rocks of the same type will look and feel different depending on where they were formed and how they were formed.

and a mineral?

A mineral has a fixed composition and a uniform structure. It forms naturally from inorganic (not plant or animal) materials. Over 4,900 minerals have been discovered. Feldspar is a mineral found in 60 per cent of rocks. Gems are mineral crystals.

What is a crystal?

A crystal is a mineral that forms into a particular shape. This is because its atoms are arranged in a three-dimensional, geometric pattern. This gives a crystal its flat faces, sharp angles and shape. Amethyst – purple crystals of the mineral quartz – form squat or tall pyramid-shaped crystals.

Squat pyramid-shaped amethyst crystals

Factfile

Types of rocks

The three rock types are grouped according to how they were made. Pressure, heat and location create a rock's grain size, texture and mineral content.

Igneous rocks

These form from liquid magma that has erupted and cooled, either slowly or quickly. Gabbro is a slow-cooled igneous rock.

Metamorphic rocks

Intense heat and/or pressure changes a rock into another type of rock. Slate is formed when clay or volcanic ash change.

Sedimentary rocks

These form when rock and organic matter sediments are compressed under water. Limestone sediment forms chalkboard chalk.

Recycling rocks

Rocks do not stay the same forever. They undergo **changes** due to weathering, **erosion**, earthquakes and volcanoes. This process is called the **rock cycle**. Igneous rocks below Earth's surface create uplifts to form mountains. **Weathering** slowly breaks down mountains into fragments and sediments. **Erosion** carries these away and **deposits** them, often into water, where they are compressed into sedimentary rocks. When exposed to **heat** and **pressure**, sedimentary rocks become metamorphic rocks, which can be heated again to form **magma** and igneous rocks.

Facts and figures

Earth's vital statistics

Greatest mass
The mantle makes up 85 per cent of the Earth's mass; the crust only one per cent.

Earth's layers
The inner core is 1,250 km wide and the outer core, 2,200 km wide. The mantle is 2,900 km wide – almost half the Earth's radius. The crust is 8–50 km deep and about 70 per cent of it is covered by ocean.

Thinnest crust
Under Lake Baikal, Russia, the world's deepest lake, the crust is only 3 km deep.

Thickest crust
This is under Mount Everest, the highest point on Earth, where it is about 65 km deep.

Largest fault
The 5,500-km Sunda Megathrust in South-East Asia caused the 2004 tsunami that killed 230,000 people.

Weathered sediments wash into the sea and waves erode rocks along Big Sur, California, USA

Boulder to pebble

Rain, wind, waves, ice, salt, plants and animals cause rocks, even the hardest ones, to weather (wear away) – boulders become pebbles, and mountains become hills.

Earth movers

Earthquakes are caused by volcanoes and the movement of tectonic plates, which causes rock masses to break and the ground to move.

The **Earth** is in **continual** change, always **weathering** and **reforming**.

Did you know?

Seismologists measure the waves of energy that are produced in an earthquake. The seismic waves are the blue lines, and the globe shows the earthquake's location.

Lava-formed black obsidian, Rainbow Mountains, Iceland

Magma on the move

Magma, which consists of liquid mantle rocks, minerals and gases from deep inside the Earth, collects in chambers and if the pressure becomes too great, an eruption will occur. Some magma will escape into vents to cool slowly; some escapes to the surface as lava in a volcanic eruption.

What's erosion?

Erosion is the process by which weathered rock fragments and sediments are moved to another place by wind, water and ice and gravity. When the transported sediments settle, it is called deposition. Monument Valley, Utah, was created from Rocky Mountain erosion that was deposited and cemented into sandstone. The sandstone weathered into towering formations.

Natural forces continue to shape Monument Valley, USA

Lithification

The process of turning deposited sediments into rock is called lithification. Fine sediments like clay become slate mostly due to compression, but larger sediments are bonded together by dissolved minerals.

Lithified rocks at Culm Measures, Cornwall, UK

Factfile

Inside the Earth

If you sliced through the Earth as though it was an onion, you would see the layers within. Rocks on the surface reveal what's happened far below.

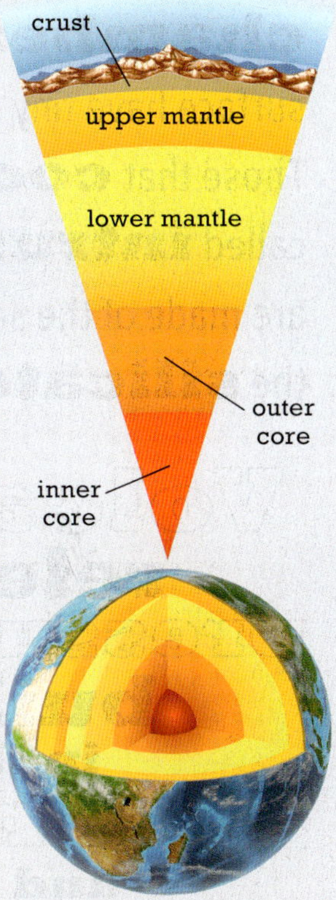

Crust

This is the outermost layer of solid rock on which we live. It consists of 10 major tectonic plates.

Mantle

The upper layer of the mantle is solid rock, while the lower layer is semi-molten rock (magma).

Outer core

Surrounding the inner core, this is an extremely hot layer of liquid iron, nickel and other elements.

Inner core

At the centre is a solid core of iron and nickel. Its high temperature makes it the 'engine room' of the Earth.

Hot rocks

Igneous rocks are without doubt Earth's rock stars! They are formed from **molten** rock that forces its way through cracks and fractures to either **erupt** onto the Earth's surface or to collect in **chambers** underground. Molten rocks that cool quickly on the surface have tiny **crystals** and are called extrusive igneous rocks. Those that **cool** slowly in chambers form larger crystals and are called **intrusive** igneous rocks. All 700 types of igneous rocks are made of the same eight **elements** that have melted to form the **silicate** minerals found in 90 per cent of the Earth's crust.

Facts and figures

Violent volcanoes

Indonesia
Since 1600, multiple volcanic eruptions in Indonesia have caused the deaths of over 160,000 people.

Iceland
When Laki, Iceland, erupted in 1783 it spewed noxious gases and lava for eight months. More than 20 per cent of the population died of famine and disease.

South America
Nevado del Ruiz, Columbia, erupted in 1985 and ejected a molten mass of rock and gas that melted a glacier. It was the glacier and mudslides that caused so much death and destruction.

Caribbean
A pyroclastic flow – a fast-moving liquid mass of rock and gas – from Mount Pelée volcano reached a temperature of 1,075°Celsius.

Volcanoes release pressure that builds up in the mantle and core.

Lava shoots hundreds of metres above Mount Etna on Sicily, Italy, during an eruption in 2013

Did you know?

Pumice is an igneous rock that is peppered with holes that are formed by bubbles of gas trapped in the magma as it rapidly cooled. Pumice is so light it can float on water.

Black sand

When lava flows into water it cools super quickly and shatters into sand-like fragments. When the flow is large enough, a black sand beach will be formed.

New landforms

The material that erupts from volcanoes changes existing landforms and creates new landforms.

Volcanic islands

Since 1918, 19 islands have formed after eruptions. Niijima appeared in November 2013 after an undersea volcanic eruption off Nishinoshima Island, Japan. The crater rose above sea level and continuing eruptions caused the growing new island to merge with the older island to the south.

Niijima – its volcano smoking – joined to the older island

Basalt columns formed by lava in the Czech Republic

An abandoned tin mine in Cornwall, UK made from granite

Basalt

Basalt is a dark, fine-grained igneous rock that contains iron and magnesium and other minerals, like quartz. Some basalts form deep in the Earth, others cool on the surface. It is abundant on Earth and on the Moon. This rock is used in construction and as ballast under railway tracks.

Granite

This important rock contains quartz, feldspars and other minerals and it can be red, pink, grey or white in colour. It is an intrusive igneous rock that cooled slowly. It is a very hard rock and it is used in construction. The King's Tomb (2,580 BCE) at Giza, Egypt, is made of red granite.

Factfile

Other igneous rocks

Igneous rocks dominate Earth's upper layers. Many, like granite, are familiar, but here are three lesser-known examples.

Pele's hair

When the wind catches strands of lava thrown into the air during an eruption, they form a volcanic glass called Pele's hair.

Ignimbrite

Consisting mostly of pumice, this pink-grey rock is formed when layers of volcanic rock and gas are compressed and cooled.

Peridotite

This olive-green rock is mined for its valuable chromium. Kimberlite, a variety of peridotite, often contains diamonds.

Rocks that change

Metamorphism is the process whereby a rock **changes** its appearance and **structure**. This happens when a rock is exposed to **heat** and pressure. Any rock – igneous, sedimentary and even **metamorphic** – can be changed into another type of rock. Heat and pressure **transforms** limestone into marble, shale or mudstone into slate and **sandstone** into quartzite. Metamorphism can occur at different **depths** and with varying amounts of heat and **pressure**. Uplift and erosion bring metamorphic rocks to the Earth's **surface**.

Facts and figures

Types of layering

Foliated rock
The thin layers form under high pressure where pressure in one direction is greater than in any other direction. This gives rocks like slate and gneiss a striped appearance.

Non-foliated rock
Dense, uniform rocks without layers – like marble and quartzite – form under low, even amounts of pressure.

Types of metamorphosis

Contact
This happens when magma bakes surrounding rocks.

Regional
When heat and pressure affect a large area, like a mountain, the entire formation changes.

Dynamic
When rocks rub against each other a powder forms that is changed by heat and pressure.

Did you know?

About 4.5 million square metres of white marble was used to clad 543 buildings in Ashgabat, Turkmenistan. This feat was rewarded with a Guinness World Record.

The Taj Mahal, India, is covered with translucent white marble

Marble cuts cleanly in any direction, so it is perfect for sculpture and construction.

Marble damage

Though marble is a dense, heavy rock, acids like lemon juice and vinegar can etch into its surface. Many ancient marble sculptures have been badly damaged by acid rain and pollution.

Just add minerals

If minerals are present in the limestone, the marble will be coloured. Serpentine creates green marble, and iron will make it red.

Naturally occurring layers of slate

Slate

This is formed when sedimentary rocks like mudstone or shale are affected by low-grade heat and pressure that cause the minerals to align at right angles to the direction of greatest pressure. This creates layers that split cleanly, leaving smooth, flat surfaces. This makes slate perfect for roof tiles and pool tables! Slate can metamorphose under different conditions into schist and gneiss.

Eclogite

Eclogite is one of the rarest metamorphic rocks and is formed under heat and pressure 50 km below the Earth's surface. This rock, made of gabbro and basalt, can contain red garnets and diamonds.

Eclogite with red garnet and green omphacite-jade crystals

Canadian gneiss with layers of pink granite and a darker iron-rich rock

Granite to gneiss

When granite or mudstone is subjected to high-grade heat and pressure, gneiss forms. Though gneiss displays layers of different minerals, it will not split cleanly like slate. Gneiss found in Canada is more than 4.03 billion years old, making it the oldest rock to be discovered on the Earth's crust.

Factfile

Other examples

Even though rocks are under intense heat and pressure, they don't melt during metamorphosis. If the rock melted it would form an igneous rock.

Schist

This metamorphic rock will split into layers, and the sample above contains shiny, flat flakes of the mineral mica.

Anthracite

This is metamorphosed coal and it is 91–98 per cent carbon. Anthracite is also known as smokeless coal or black diamond.

Quartzite

When quartz sandstone is affected by high heat and pressure, quartzite will be formed. Quartzite is a hard-wearing rock.

Layer upon layer

Sedimentary rock is made from **igneous**, metamorphic and other sedimentary rocks. The weathered **sediments** of these rocks are carried away by **wind**, water, ice, or earthquakes and deposited, usually in **layers** underwater, and then compacted. The layers often include decayed **plants** and dead animals. Some sedimentary rocks are fine-grained, like **chert**; others, like conglomerate, contain small stones and **shells**. Dissolved minerals **cement** the sediments together. Some sedimentary rocks found in **Greenland** are 3.9 billion years old!

Facts and figures

How do we use sedimentary rocks?

Bauxite
The ore from which aluminium is extracted.

Conglomerate
This rock is crushed for use in the construction industry.

Dolomite
Can be used as a soil conditioner, in livestock feed and in the making of glass, ceramics, bricks and chemicals.

Flint
Used as fire-starters and building material.

Iron ore
Used to make steel.

Pumice
An abrasive used in soaps and nail files.

Quartz sand
Used to make glass.

Shale
Source of liquid and gaseous hydrocarbons (fuel).

What's $CaCO_3$?

This is the symbol for calcium carbonate – chalk. Chalk forms underwater from calcite shells. It is soft enough to write with, but hard enough to form the White Cliffs of Dover, UK.

Rock cycle

When a soft sedimentary rock like shale is affected by heat and pressure, it changes to slate, which is a harder metamorphic rock.

A 'marble cake' of coloured sandstones at White Pocket, Arizona, USA

Did you know?

Uluru in Australia's Northern Territory was formed 550 million years ago under a sea, but now rises 348 metres above the ground. Millennia of weathering has shaped this monolith.

The rose-red Treasury (Al Khazneh) building at Petra, Jordan

Red sandstone

This sandstone, often called Nubian sandstone, is found in north-eastern Africa, and is the rock into which the city of Petra was carved over 2,000 years ago. It is red or brown, but can exhibit a rainbow of colours. Sandstone is crushed to make building sand, cut into blocks, carved for sculpture and ground for glass production.

Coal

This fossil fuel was formed 300 million years ago from dead plant matter that was compacted to form peat and eventually coal. Coal is mostly carbon, and has been burned to provide heat since 2,000 BCE. Coal is a non-renewable resource.

Peat is cut into blocks and dried for use as fuel in Ireland

As rings in a tree tell its story, layers of rock reveal Earth's timeline.

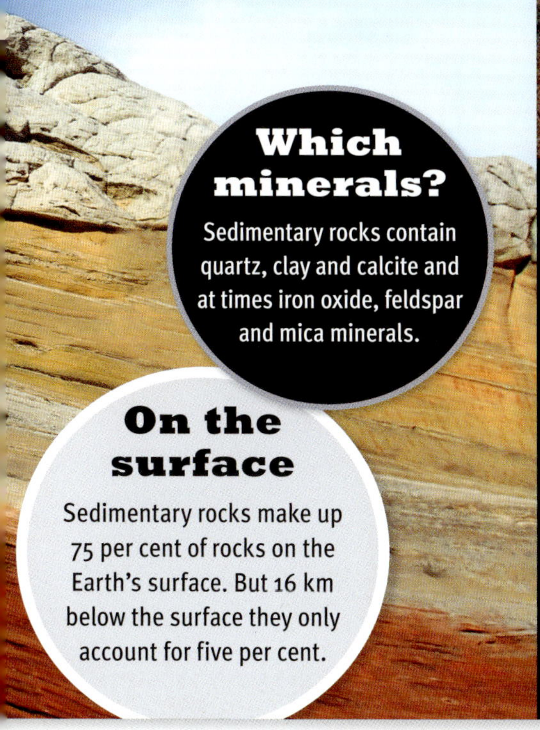

Which minerals?

Sedimentary rocks contain quartz, clay and calcite and at times iron oxide, feldspar and mica minerals.

On the surface

Sedimentary rocks make up 75 per cent of rocks on the Earth's surface. But 16 km below the surface they only account for five per cent.

Sun-dried evaporites

These form when a liquid containing dissolved chemical sediments, dry up (evaporate) under the sun's heat. Halite, or rock salt, is an evaporite. It is normally white, but impurities will colour it. More than just a food flavouring and road de-icer, salt has 14,000 other industrial uses.

Impurities or a bacteria turned this rock salt orange

Stories in stone

Fossils are the remains or imprints of animals and plants that lived **thousands** to billions of years ago. The hardest parts of the animal, like **bone** and shell, have the greatest chance of surviving as fossils. But whether it is a fossil of a **paw** print (a trace fossil) or a complete **skeleton**, they open a window on Earth's history. Fossils have been found on every **continent** on Earth, mostly in sedimentary rock. The most recently **uncovered** fossil hotspot is in Liaoning Province, China, where **palaeontologists** have discovered fossils of five, feathered **dinosaur** species.

Facts and figures

Latin word
Fossil is a Latin word meaning 'dug up'.

Fireball!
Without fossils we would never have known about dinosaurs, but they also tell us why dinosaurs perished 65 million years ago. In the rocks where dinosaur fossils have been found, there is evidence of a fireball and suffocating dust clouds that were caused by an asteroid hitting Earth.

No bone
Fossil bone does not contain bone, only the minerals that replaced it during fossilisation.

The oldest dinosaur
A 230 million-year-old prosauropod fossil was found in Madagascar, off Africa.

The largest dinosaur
A *Sauroposeidon* fossil showed this species was 18 metres tall and weighed as much as nine elephants.

Fossil of a marine reptile (ichthyosaur) from the Jurassic period, 201–145 million years ago

There is a one in a million chance of an animal fossilising.

Stone or bone?

Stones are often mistaken for bone fossils. A stone will look the same inside and outside, whereas the inside of a bone fossil contains channels and tiny holes.

Ancient dung

Coprolites are fossilised animal dung, and they reveal what animals were eating. Coprolites are rare as poo decays quickly.

Did you know?

The oldest fossils are 3.2 billion-year-old algae. Layers of algae build up to form mounds called stromatolites. This stromatolite in Western Australia is 3,000 years old and still growing!

Mary Anning

Born in 1799 in a seaside town in Dorset, UK, Mary taught herself about geology and she found the first complete marine reptile fossil on what is now called the Jurassic Coast. To earn money, Anning's family sold the fossils that Mary collected from a table near a coach stop at an inn.

Fossilised plants

Plant fossils provide information about Earth's history. Fossils indicate that Antarctica, for example, was once thickly carpeted with rainforest, and rocks from Greenland show evidence of global warming over 200 million years ago! Coal and oil were formed by fossilised plants.

Trilobite fossils like the ones that Anning found and sold

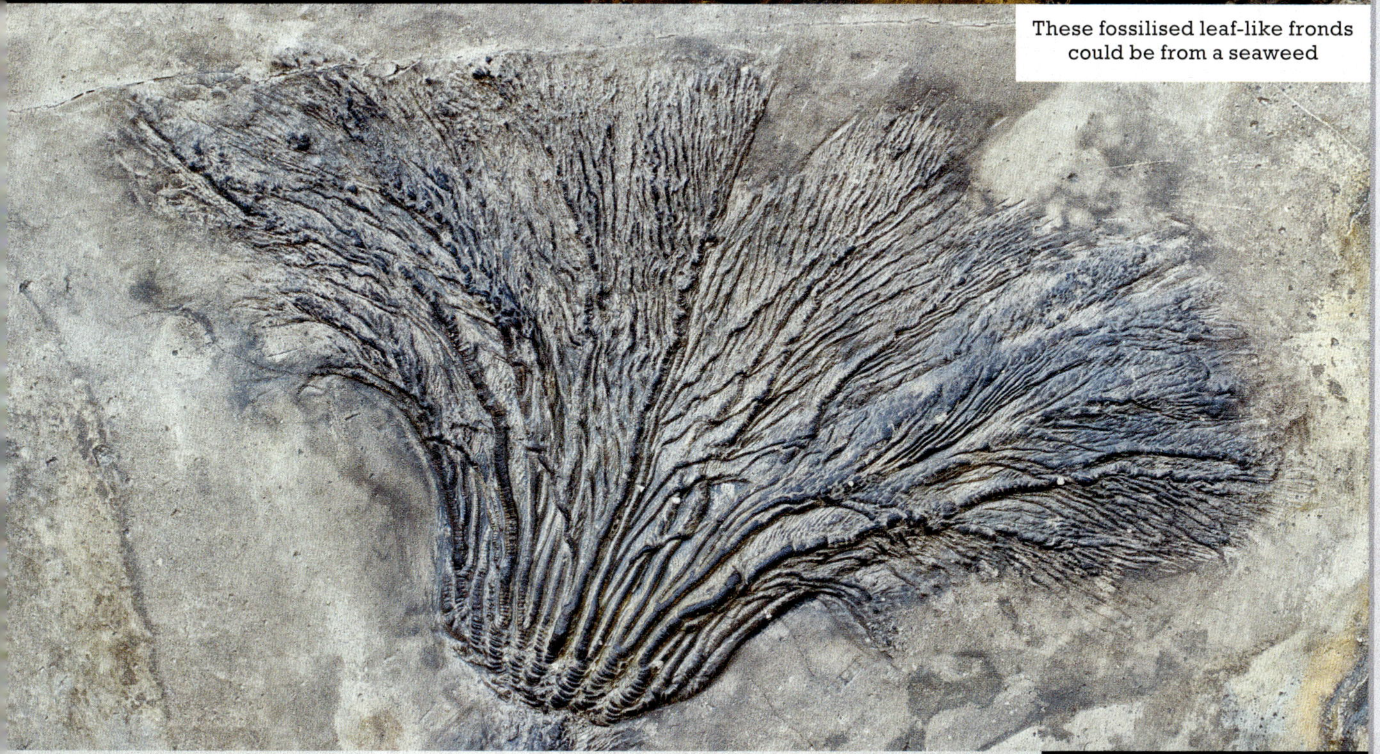

These fossilised leaf-like fronds could be from a seaweed

Flies and a bee preserved in two amber gems

Preserved in amber

All trees produce a resin and when the resin is fossilised it is called amber. Since Neolithic times (commencing 10,200 BCE) amber has been prized as a gemstone, but to fossil hunters it is prized for the animals and plants that were trapped and preserved in the resin.

Factfile

Fossil formation

Stage one
Fossilisation can occur if an animal dies in sand, mud or water, the corpse is not scavenged and the temperature is very low.

Stage two
The corpse is covered by sediment that will slow but not stop skin and organs decaying. Bones and shells are more resilient.

Stage three
Layers of sediment compress over the corpse and form rock. Minerals soak down to preserve or dissolve the skeleton.

Stage four
The rock weathers, exposing the preserved skeleton, a mineral mould of the skeleton or an imprint of the skeleton.

Remarkable rocks

Our planet contains an array of **amazing** rock formations. Some are even **hidden** beneath our feet! These beautiful caverns, etched over **millennia** by slightly acidic water seeping through **limestone**, are otherworldly and strange. Then there are those places where natural **forces** have carved rock into fantastical shapes, created **multi-coloured** landscapes or **chasms** so deep that they seem bottomless. But while we gaze at these wonders that appear **permanent** but aren't, Earth is constantly making and **transforming** rocks.

Facts and figures

Highest elevation
When the Indian tectonic plate pushed against the Asian plate, they formed Mount Everest, which continues growing 25 mm each year.

Deepest gorge
As plates forced the Himalayas in Nepal higher, a river sliced through the uplift creating Kali Gandaki Gorge. This gorge sits 5,500 metres below the surrounding peaks.

Lowest elevation
The Dead Sea is 400 metres below sea level and was formed when two tectonic plates spread apart, causing a 'dip' in the crust.

Deepest trench
At 10,994 metres below sea level lies Challenger Deep in the Mariana Trench, Western Pacific Ocean. This trench was created when a tectonic plate curved down as it pushed up against another tectonic plate.

Jeita Caves, Lebanon, has a world-record stalactite that hangs 8.2 metres from the cave roof

Did you know?

Limestone formations caused by dripping water are known as dripstones. A column is formed when the lowest tip of a stalactite meets the topmost tip of a stalagmite.

Illegal trade

Growing less than 10 cm in 1,000 years, it is illegal in most countries to collect, mine or sell stalagmites and stalactites.

Drip by drip

When water drips into a cave, each drip leaves a tiny amount of mineral (calcite) on the cave roof. These form into stalactites. When drips hit the floor, the minerals build a stalagmite.

Stalactites and stalagmites are sometimes referred to collectively as dripstone.

Troll's Tongue with a glacial valley in the background

Troll's Tongue

Jutting 700 metres above a glacial valley in Norway, this narrow horizontal rock shelf was created when water from an Ice Age glacier froze and expanded in cracks in the mountain. This eventually caused a huge chunk of gneiss rock to break off, leaving behind what the Norwegian locals call Trolltunga.

Some of the formations in the Shilin Stone Forest are 30 metres tall

Stone forest

The Shilin Stone Forest area was a vast expanse of sea about 270 million years ago, but movement of the tectonic plates caused an uplift that forced the water to retreat. The exposed limestone weathered over millions of years to create these amazing formations, some of which resemble animals, trees and humans.

The Wave is on unmarked path in the middle of a hot wilderness

The Wave

The colourful U-shaped troughs were formed by water carving deeper and deeper into the sandstone during the Jurassic Age. When the water stopped flowing, wind continued to weather and shape this extraordinary place in Arizona, USA.

Factfile

Nature's rock sculptures

The forces that shape the Earth are movement of the tectonic plates, volcanic eruptions, weathering, erosion and deposition.

Ball's Pyramid

The world's tallest stack, off Australia in the Pacific Ocean, is 551 metres high. Only 0.5 per cent of the original volcano remains.

Pancake Rocks

These formations in New Zealand are the weathered remains of compressed limestone, separated by layers of softer mud.

Nakalele Blowhole

This Hawaiian blowhole formed when waves wore a hole in a cave roof. When a wave enters the cave it blasts up through the hole.

Hard-working rocks

Humans have used rocks since **ancient** times for buildings, tools, jewellery and **sculpture**. Rocks have also been used in dyes, **medicines**, cosmetics and even evil deeds! Ancient Egyptians sprinkled coffins with **hematite** to make any grave robbers sneeze. Persians knew that **arsenic** was a powerful poison. Minerals are in almost everything we **use** and consume. All these valuable **resources** are extracted from inside the Earth. It is estimated that 22,000 kg of rocks and **minerals** are required **annually** to meet the needs of one American citizen.

Facts and figures

Useful rocks and minerals

Every day we use or consume things that are made using rocks or minerals.

Batteries: lead, lithium
Bike handlebars: zinc (used to make chrome)
Cat litter: zeolites
Computer chips: silica
Cola can: bauxite
Fireworks: sulphur
Fizzy drinks: phosphate
Jeans: pumice (to distress the denim)
Light bulbs: tungsten, molybdenite
Mirror: silver
Pencils: graphite
Plastic bottle: crude oil
Sandwich bread: trona (baking soda)
Shoes: chromite (used in tanning)
Sparkly make up: mica
Tea mug: clay
Toothpaste: fluorite, pumice, kaolinite, titanium

Eroding the Earth

Mining for rocks and minerals moves more earth than erosion. To make one tonne of copper, over 125 tonnes of copper ore are dug out of the ground.

Non-renewable

Minerals are non-renewable resources because they take millions of years to form and can't be replaced during a person's life.

Easter Island's ancient statues, called moai, are made from volcanic tuff.

Layers of sediment have left only the heads of the moai exposed

Did you know?

Iron-rich lodestones are magnetic rocks. In ancient times they were thought to have magical powers. They were the first compasses – the name lodestone meaning 'course stone'.

Native American Indian flint arrowheads and spear point

Ancient tools

Humans have been shaping tools and weapons from stone, usually flint, since the Stone Age, some 2.6 million years ago. When flint – a hard, glassy sedimentary rock – is hit it splits to remove a 'flake'. Repeated hitting will create sharp edges for an axe, spear or arrowhead.

The greatest wall

The Great Wall of China is the longest wall and largest piece of ancient architecture in the world. The wall is built of granite and kiln-fired bricks, but some sections used rammed earth, limestone and marble. One hundred million tonnes of material was used during its 2,000-years of construction.

Coal power

When coal is burned, the energy in the organic matter (dead plants) is released. This energy can heat water to produce steam that can drive a turbine to generate electricity. Over 40 per cent of electricity is produced using coal, releasing excessive carbon dioxide (CO_2) into the air.

The Great Wall of China at Mutianyu is constructed of granite

A coal-fired power plant producing electricity

Factfile

Building materials

Construction uses more of Earth's resources than any industry, but building materials have changed little in over 5,000 years.

Glass

First made in 2,500 BCE, it is produced by heating sand to 1,700°Celsius. Glass can clad buildings from top to bottom.

Brick

Bricks of sand, mud and water have been in use since 8,000 BCE. Yemen's mud brick flats were the world's first skyscrapers.

Concrete

Tenerife's Auditorio is built of concrete, which is a mixture of water, gravel, sand, chalk and clay. It is a relatively new material.

Crystals

Crystals are solid materials in which the atoms – the building blocks of all matter – are arranged in a regular **pattern**. This pattern is **repeated** over and over again as the crystal grows. As its simplest, a crystal has **flat** surfaces (faces) and sharp edges. The rate at which **magma** cools determines the size of a crystal – rapid **cooling** means small crystals while slow cooling allows large crystals to form. No wonder we have found **shiny**, mirror-like crystals fascinating – they are not only **beautiful** but they are some of Earth's **oldest** and most colourful secrets.

Facts and figures

Six crystal shapes

Cubic crystals
Equal sides meet at right angles.
Examples: diamond, pyrite

Triclinic crystals
All sides are of different lengths and none meet at right angles.
Examples: turquoise, feldspar

Orthorhombic crystals
Similar to monoclinic.
Example: topaz

Monoclinic crystals
4 vertical sides not meeting at right angles.
Example: azurite

Hexagonal crystals
These have 6 vertical sides meeting at 60 degree angles that are often topped by a 6-sided pyramid.
Example: amethyst

Tetragonal crystals
A rectangular prism with square top and bottom.
Example: rutile

Quartz crystals have six faces topped with a six-sided pyramid

Frozen solid

The ancient Greek for crystal, *kystallos*, means icy cold. It was thought that clear quartz was ice frozen so hard it would never melt.

Crystals that melt

Snowflakes are ice crystals that start life as a six-sided crystal prism, but then grow six arms. All ice crystals are unique and most are not perfectly symmetrical.

Did you know?

There is a theory that at the centre of the Earth is a crystal of solid iron about the size of our moon. Though temperatures here should melt the iron, extreme pressure prevents it.

Temperature, pressure, space and chemical conditions affect crystal growth.

Blue-green agate microcrystals and white quartz crystals in geodes

Hidden beauty

Geodes are hollow rocks formed from an air bubble in volcanic rocks or in holes left by decayed plants. The shell around the 'hole' hardens and mineral-rich water trickles through depositing minerals that become tiny microcrystals. These form layers in the geode or grow into larger crystals.

Oldest crystal

In 2001 a sheep station at Jack Hills, Western Australia, yielded up a tiny zircon crystal 4.4 billion years old. It is the earliest sample of the Earth's crust yet discovered. This crystal proves there was water and possibly life on the young planet Earth all those billions of years ago.

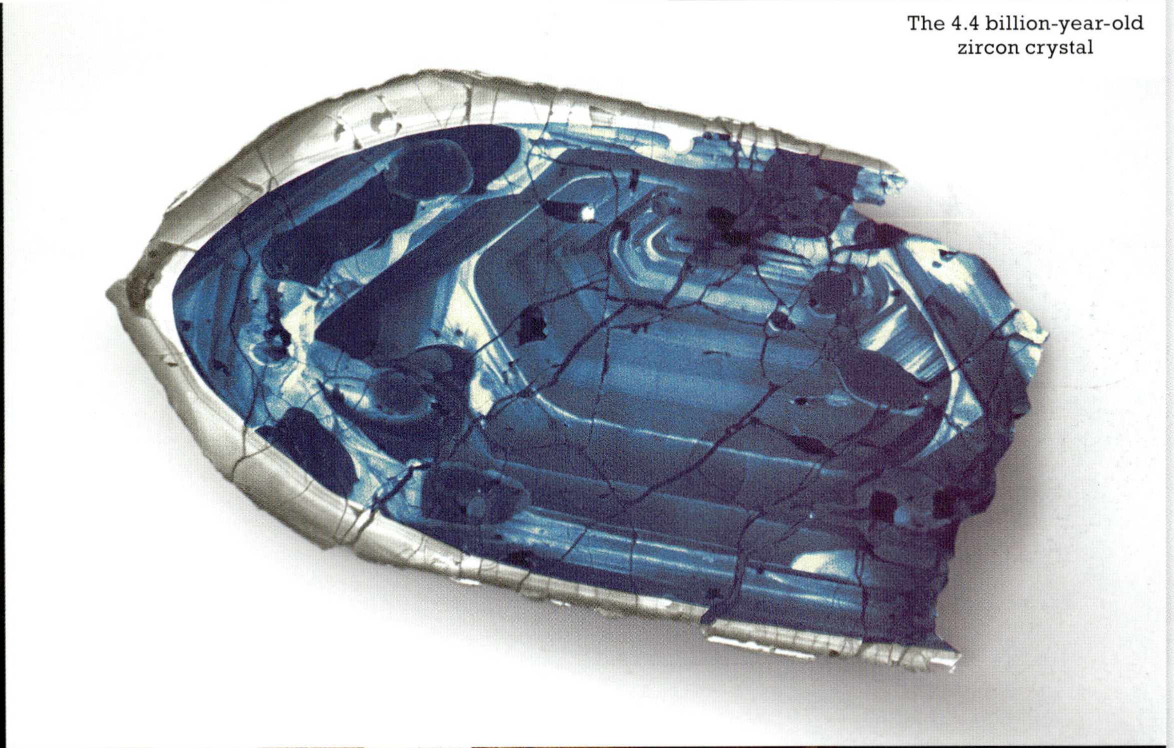

The 4.4 billion-year-old zircon crystal

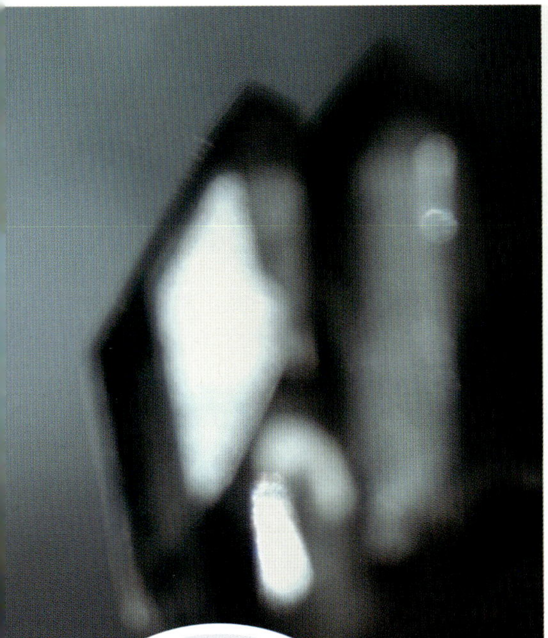

Edible crystals

Salt crystals are cube-shaped (cubic) and sugar crystals and menthol crystals (as used in chewing gum) are six-sided (hexagonal) columns.

Don't be fooled

Glass is a not a crystal. Even though it can have flat faces and sharp angles it is a non-crystalline material.

The amazing Cave of Crystals, Mexico

Giant crystals

Mexico's Cave of Crystals contains 11-metre-long crystals. Lying 1.6 km underground with a consistent 58°Celsius temperature, the caves provided 500,000 years of perfect crystal-growing conditions. Growth would have continued but the water level was lowered by mistake in 1985.

Crystal know-how

The internal **structure** of a molecule gives a crystal its shape, colour, **texture** and cleavage (how it splits), plus it determines its hardness and how it **interacts** with light. With the invention of the **scanning** tunneling microscope (STM) in 1981, scientists were finally able to see the individual **atoms** in a crystal and the repeated **pattern** that they form. Naturally-formed crystals are rarely perfect – an atom may be **missing** from the pattern, an **impurity** present or the temperature changed during crystal formation – but **imperfections** just add to their appeal.

Facts and figures

How to identify a crystal

These are a few of the tests crystallographers use to work out which crystal is which.

Colour
Identifying by colour alone can be unreliable as impurities can affect colour and minerals can occur in various colours.

Cleavage
Crystals will split along lines of weakness.

Fluorescence
Some crystals glow under UV light.

Hardness
Mohs' scale of hardness shows the relative hardness of minerals.

Streak
The colour of the powder produced by a crystal when rubbed on a rough surface.

Acid test
How a crystal reacts when treated with acid.

Crystals are repeated three-dimensional patterns of atoms.

A rare and valuable emerald crystal embedded in a rock containing calcite crystals

Did you know?

Diamond and graphite (as used in pencils) are both carbon, but graphite atoms are in sheets that slide against each other, and diamond atoms are in an interlocked 3D lattice.

Rarest crystal

Painite was for many decades the world's rarest crystal with only two known samples. Even with recent discoveries, this red gem is still extremely rare and highly sought.

Crystal experts

Crystallographers study the structure and properties of crystals. Until X-rays were invented, rulers were used to measure crystals!

Butterfly twinned crystals of calcite

Twinning

When similar crystals grow from a shared point in different directions, it is called twinning. It is caused by an error during crystallisation. Quartz, calcite, fluorite, gypsum and cinnabar are just a few minerals that 'twin'. Twinned crystals can form various shapes, some resemble fishtails, butterflies and even stars.

Desert rose

These curious and beautiful formations are found in dry, sandy places because the conditions allow the minerals (gypsum or barite and sand) to form flattened crystals that look like petals. Desert roses are 1.3–10 cm across, but one grew to 43 cm.

A fragile gypsum desert rose

Spot the difference

It can be difficult to identify crystals simply by looking at their colour and shape. Testing though would show that these two crystals are very different. Topaz and yellow-orange citrine look similar in their natural and cut and polished states, so citrine gemstones are often passed off as the more valuable topaz.

The rare and valuable red-orange topaz

The less valuable citrine

Factfile

Mohs' scale of hardness

Developed in 1812 by Friedrich Mohs, this test compares the resistance of a mineral when scratched by 10 reference minerals.

Talc: hardness one

This is the softest mineral so it will not make a definite groove on any harder minerals. Talc is softer than a fingernail.

Apatite: hardness five

This middle-ranking mineral will scratch softer minerals, but leave harder ones unscratched. Glass is harder than apatite.

Diamond: hardness 10

This is the hardest of all minerals and will leave a scratch on just about everything other than two man-made materials.

Colourful crystals

Colourful crystals are always in demand as they can be cut and **polished** to create beautiful gems. Gems are used to make jewellery or other adornments. Crystals **grown** under perfect conditions have a **consistent** appearance and colour and are ideal for making into **gems**. In nature, though, growing conditions are often less than perfect so a crystal may **lack** colour or be flawed. But when a crystal is out of the ground it can be **artificially** altered to improve it. A colourless **topaz** turns blue when exposed to radiation, and **heating** will make a red ruby even redder.

Facts and figures

Birthstones

Each month has a gem – called a birthstone. Most score highly on the Mohs Hardness Scale (MHS).

Jan: Red garnet. MHS: 6.5–7.5

Feb: Violet amethyst. MHS: 7

Mar: Blue aquamarine. MHS: 7.5–8

Apr: Colourless diamond. MHS: 10

May: Green Emerald. MHS: 7.5–8

June: Pearl. MHS: 2.5–4.5

July: Red ruby. MHS: 9

Aug: Green peridot. MHS: 6.5–7

Sept: Blue sapphire. MHS: 9

Oct: Multi-coloured opal. MHS: 5.5–6

Nov: Colourless topaz. MHS: 8

Dec: Blue-green turquoise. MHS: 5–7

Of 3,800 minerals, humans only find 100 alluring enough to be gems.

Purple amethyst, citrine and other coloured quartz crystals

Clear or frosted?

Transparent minerals, like purest diamond, allow light to pass as it does through clear glass. Translucent ones are like frosted glass, only letting some light through.

Light blocked

An opaque mineral does not let any light pass through. Lapis lazuli, jet, jadeite, turquoise and obsidian are opaque gems.

Did you know?

Sapphires can be blue (the most valuable), white, green, yellow, orange, pink, purple, brown, black, colourless and colour changing. A red 'sapphire' is a ruby.

Quartz

This mineral makes up 12 per cent of the Earth's crust and is a compound of silicon and oxygen. Pure quartz is colourless and transparent and its six-sided crystal is topped with a pyramid. Some quartz crystals are large, but those in agate are almost invisible. Sandstone contains quartz.

Light plays tricks

A crystal get its colour from chemicals in its environment, but how we 'see' that colour is a 'trick' of the light. Daylight contains many colours, and when it hits a crystal (or any object), most of the light is absorbed but the bit that is reflected is what we see. If red is reflected, we will see a red crystal.

Large white quartz crystals

Red fluorite reflects red light

Green fluorite reflects green light

Glowing in the dark

About 15 per cent of minerals can absorb light and then release light of a different wavelength, which means we see the mineral change colour. This is fluorescence. Minerals can fluoresce up to five colours. If white fluorite is exposed to sunlight and moved to shade, it will glow blue-violet for a few moments.

Fluorite fluorescing under ultraviolet (UV) light

Factfile

Quartz of many colours

Quartz is the most varied of all minerals and occurs in at least 24 colours and forms. It has been used in jewellery since antiquity.

Rose quartz

Varying from light pink to rosy red, its colour may come from minerals where it was formed or natural exposure to radiation.

Smoky quartz

This grey-brown to almost black quartz can be transparent, translucent or opaque. Its colouring is due to natural radiation.

Green quartz

A green mineral has coloured these phantom quartz crystals. A phantom crystal has the outline of a smaller crystal inside.

Gems and jewellery

Adorning ourselves with jewellery started over **100,000** years ago when Neanderthals strung eagle talons onto **sinew**. The first 'jewels' were stones, shells, **wood**, animal skins, feathers and bones, and it was the ancient societies of Egypt, **India** and China that developed the skills to use precious metals and minerals, like **gold**, silver, lapis lazuli and emerald, and to give them **artistic** and symbolic value. **Jewellery** has always been worn for the same reasons: to show wealth and express **love**. From the first foraged 'jewels' grew a large jewellery **industry** worth many billions of pounds a year.

Facts and figures

Perfect diamond
The Strawn-Wagner Diamond is unique in scoring 0/0/0, indicating no flaws in cut, colour or clarity. It was mined in Arkansas, USA, in 1990.

Largest opal
The Olympic Australis weighs 3,450 grams and is 99 per cent gem quality. It was found in Coober Pedy, South Australia in 1956. It remains uncut.

Most expensive auction jewel
A pink diamond, known as the Graff Pink, was discovered in the 1950s. It was sold for £29 million, breaking all auction records for a single gem.

Rarest jewel
Though hotly contested, the Smithsonian Alexandrite weighing 68.05 carats is the world's rarest jewel. It changes from green-blue to pink-red under different lighting.

Gold crystal

Single crystals of gold, silver and platinum are rare, but in 1914 a single crystal of gold – the size of a golf ball – was found in South America.

Space gems

Meteorites and impactites (rocks modified by impact with meteorites) can be cut and polished to make gems. These gems that fall from the sky are very rare and valuable.

The Crown Jewels are priceless because of their history, not their gemstones.

St Edward's crown is the oldest and most important piece in the British Crown Jewels

Did you know?

Since ancient times gems have been valued for their healing properties. Emerald was believed to cure cholera and malaria, and powdered lapis lazuli was mixed with milk to treat boils.

Red corundum, blue sapphires and red rubies

Gemstone corundum

This mineral, a compound of aluminium and oxygen, is a ruby in its red form and a sapphire in other colours. The red and blue varieties occur when chromium or iron and titanium are present. These crystals may be heated to improve their colour when used as gemstones in jewellery.

Turban pin (1600s) with emeralds and rubies

An ancient jadeite pendant from Mexico

Soothing emerald

This green gem has 'soothed souls and excited imaginations since antiquity', which is why Egyptian slaves worked mines to find them for Cleopatra and why the 10-cm Mogul Mughal Emerald is inscribed with prayer texts. A high quality emerald is more valuable and desirable than a diamond.

Non-crystal gems

Gems that have no crystal pattern or set chemical composition are known as mineraloids. Jadeite and opal are mineraloids. Jadeite can be white through to green and even pink. Opals can display a rainbow of colours in each sample, with black opals being the rarest.

A rough opal and a polished opal stone

Factfile

Organic gems

These gems are produced by living organisms or from their decay. Many organic gems are so rare or threatened that their use in jewellery is prohibited.

Jet

This black rock is a form of coal and is made when woody material is buried in sediment where it decays and is then heated.

Coral

Coral is formed by tiny organisms that excrete calcium carbonate to form hard white, red and even black tree-like structures.

Pearls

When a grain of sand is trapped in a mollusc's shell, the mollusc covers it in nacre, and layer by layer a natural pearl is formed.

Diamonds

Highly valued for their beauty and **durability**, diamonds have come to **symbolise** enduring love. It was long thought that decaying plant matter produced the **carbon** from which diamonds **formed**, but we now know they were formed over 3,000 million years ago, long before the appearance of **plants**. Scientists are unsure of how long it takes a **diamond** to grow, but the largest one to survive violent ejection from the Earth is the **Cullinan**. This 62 kg rough diamond was cut to form nine main **gems**. Two of these valuable gems are in the **Crown Jewels**, London.

Facts and figures

Diamond discoveries

400 BCE–1700s
India is the only producer of diamonds.

1725
Diamonds discovered in Brazil, South America.

1840s
Diamonds are found in the USA.

1871
Discovery of the 83.5 carat Star of South Africa in South Africa.

1908–1967
Diamonds found in nine other African countries.

1950s
Diamonds discovered in Russia and in the gold fields of Australia.

1991
Canadian diamonds mined from frozen rock.

1990s onwards
It becomes known that diamonds, called blood diamonds, are funding wars in Africa.

Brilliant round cut diamonds have 58-facets, or faces

Did you know?

The blue Hope Diamond, seen here in its latest setting, was mined in the 17th century and has been owned by royalty, stolen, recut, bought and sold. It is thought to bring bad luck.

Invincible gemstone

The word diamond comes from the ancient Greek, *adamas*, which means indestructible and invincible. These words describe the extreme hardness of diamonds.

Grading diamonds

In the 1950s the 4Cs standard was introduced to grade all diamonds. The 4Cs are colour, clarity, cut and carat.

A natural diamond embedded in a kimberlite rock

Billions of atoms

When carbon is subjected to temperatures of 1,050°Celsius at depths of 150 km in the Earth's mantle, it will form diamond crystals. It takes billion and billions of carbon atoms to lock together to form a one-carat diamond. The diamonds are brought to the surface in vertical tubes, called kimberlite pipes, in an eruption.

Types of mining

There are many ways to mine for diamonds. From tunnelling underground shafts to searching the earth removed from huge holes. Sometimes riverbeds are dug up for diamonds or seabeds can be drilled for diamond-containing material.

Using explosives to loosen rock in an open cut diamond mine

Not the real thing

Cubic zirconia is made in a laboratory and though it looks and sparkles like a diamond, it is much more affordable.

Natural flaws

The clarity of a diamond relates to the number and types of flaws or marks inside the gem.

Fewer than one in a million rough diamonds are large enough to produce a one-carat gem.

Cutting edge

About 70 per cent of diamonds are industrial diamonds (bort). These diamonds are not of gem quality. Because of its hardness, diamond is used as an abrasive in cutting and drilling. Diamonds are also used in radiation equipment, lasers, computer disk drives and electrical circuits.

The diamond-encrusted tip of a dentist's drill

Crystals at work

Crystals are used in almost every type of modern **technology**. It was the discovery in the 1880s that **crystals** behave in very **predictable** ways when heated that made the 'Information Age' possible. The use of crystals in **jewellery** is small in comparison to their **use** in industry, science and technology. To fulfil the demand, crystals are grown in **laboratories**. A synthetic 32-carat diamond crystal can be **grown** in 300 hours; it would take **billions** of years to form naturally. Crystals have even been grown in the **orbiting** International Space Station!

Facts and figures

The importance of crystals

Solar cells
Solar cells convert light energy into electrical energy using wafers of crystalline silicon. Solar cells power anything from calculators and garden lights to orbiting space stations.

Liquid crystals
Liquid crystals are used in digital displays (LCDs) in wristwatches, calculators, medical diagnostic tools and more. Liquid crystals in glass control how much sunlight passes through. The first liquid crystal was extracted from a carrot in 1888!

Semiconductors
Semiconductors, usually crystalline silicon or germanium, are used in electronic circuits to control electrical current, and without them there would be no Internet, tablets or smartphones.

Did you know?

Natural crystals often contain impurities, but synthetic crystals can be flawless. Synthetic bismuth crystals grow quickly at the edges creating an incredible stepped shape.

Electronic circuit boards rely on a crystal vibrating at a precise frequency

You'll **find** crystals in **salt** and **sugar**, LCD **displays** and silicon **chips**!

Crystal navigation

A homing pigeon's great sense of direction may be due to microscopic crystals of magnetite in its beak. These help it navigate using Earth's magnetic fields.

Kitchen crystals

Bismuth has a low melting point, so synthetic bismuth crystals can be grown in minutes on a household stove!

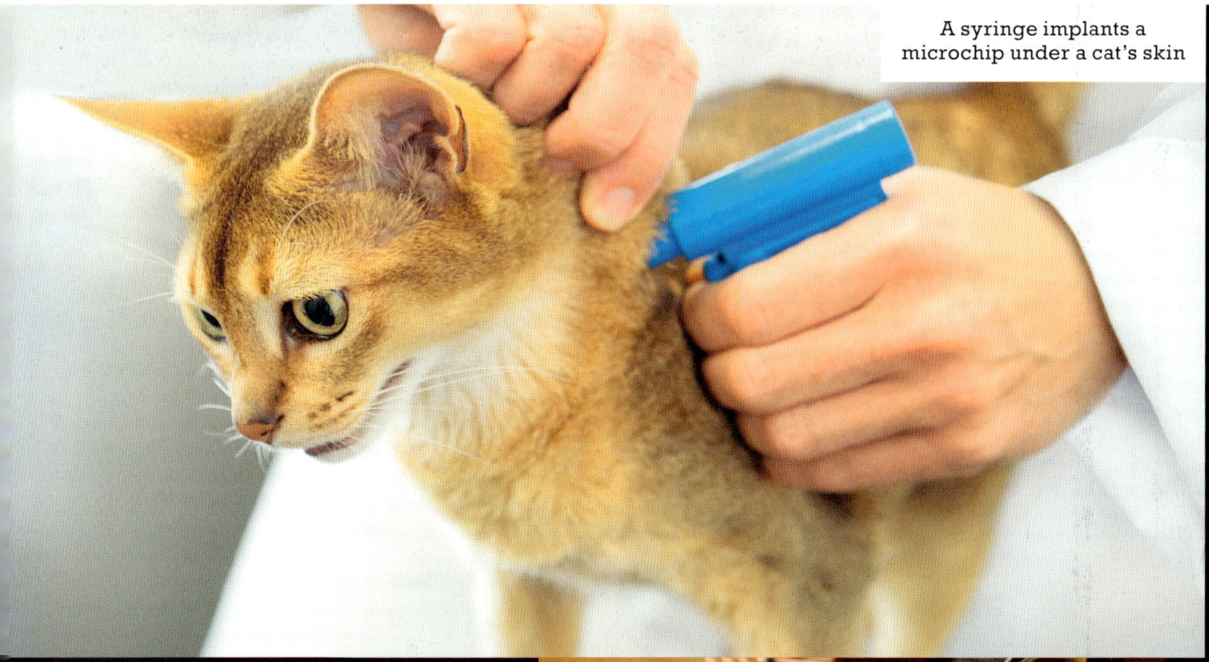

A syringe implants a microchip under a cat's skin

Tiny microchips

The size of a grain of rice, a microchip is a silicon crystal circuit that can be implanted in people and animals. In medicine, microchip implants can deliver drugs at the right time and quantity to patients. Implanted into a pet, a microchip means a lost pet can be returned to its owner.

Crystal radio

In the early 20th century it was discovered that crystalline minerals could be used to pick up radio signals. A crystal detector, connected by a wire, was used in crystal radios. These simple machines heralded the origin of electronics, and today a crystal detector would be called a diode.

A crystal radio with two mineral samples to be used as detectors

Harder diamonds

Most industrial diamonds are lab-grown, and some are harder than natural diamonds.

Healing power

The first use of crystals dates back to 400 BCE in ancient Sumeria (now Iraq). The crystals were used in magic potions.

Quartz crystals for industrial use growing in an autoclave

Synthetic crystals

Laboratory-made crystals are essentially identical to natural crystals. In the melt process, chemicals are dropped through a flame. The melted material collects on a rotating plate and forms a crystal. They can also be made in an autoclave – a steel drum that mimics natural crystal-growing conditions.

Glossary

Aggregate
Rocks and sediment cemented together.

Bedrock
The solid layer of rock under the Earth's uppermost loose surface of soil, clay, gravel, sand and rock fragments.

Cave
A naturally formed chamber in a mountain or cliff on land or in the sea.

Cleavage
The shape that occurs when a rock or mineral splits along planes.

Crystal
A solid where the smallest particles (atoms) are arranged in a geometrical pattern to form flat faces and sharp angles.

Earthquake
Movement of the crust, usually at a fault line, which causes the ground to shake.

Earth's core
Two layers at the very centre of the Earth make up the core, which is very hot and consists of iron and nickel metals.

Earth's crust
This is the outermost layer of solid rock on which we live. It is made up of rocks and minerals.

Element
A substance made up of identical atoms. An element is the simplest substance and cannot be broken down.

Erosion
The process of moving weathered rock and sediment by wind, water or ice (glaciers).

Extrusive rock
A volcanic rock that cools on the Earth's surface.

Fault
A crack in the Earth's crust, often between tectonic plates, which moves over time.

Fossil
A fossil is the preserved remains or traces of a living organism from the distant past.

Geologist
A scientist who studies the Earth's structure and its history.

Glacier
A large, slowly moving body of ice.

Hardness scale
The resistance of minerals when they are scratched by another mineral.

Ice Age
A period of time in Earth's history of long-term freezing temperatures resulting in the formation of large sheets of ice.

Igneous rock
A rock formed through the cooling of magma or lava.

Intrusive rock
Volcanic rock that cools below the Earth's surface.

Lava
Lava is molten rock that is expelled to the Earth's surface by a volcano.

Lustre
How light reflects off a rock or mineral.

Magma
Molten rock that is under the Earth's surface.

Mantle
This layer lies between the Earth's outer crust and the core. It is made mostly of silicate rocks.

Metamorphic rock
A rock that is changed by intense heat and/or pressure into another type of rock.

Mineral
A naturally occurring material with a set composition and a uniform structure. A mineral is often a combination of two or more elements.

Mountain
A landform that rises above the surrounding land caused by tectonic plates moving towards one another to form volcanoes that erupt or cause uplifts.

Rock
A rock is naturally formed when one or more minerals or non-minerals clump together into a solid lump.

Rock cycle
The continual process where 'new' rocks are made from rocks that already exist.

Sand
Loose, medium-fine particles weathered from rocks or minerals.

Sediment
Any material that results from weathering and decomposition. It is carried by erosion to bodies of water where it settles on the bottom.

Sedimentary rock
Rocks formed when layers of sediment are pressed and cemented together.

Seismic waves
Waves of energy released by earthquakes or volcanoes that travel through the Earth.

Strata
Layers or bands in rocks.

Tectonic plates
Large sections of the Earth's crust that move.

Volcanic
Anything caused or created by a volcano.

Volcano
An opening in the crust through which molten rock (magma) erupts to the surface as lava.

Weathering
The wearing away and breaking down of rocks and landforms, such as cliffs and mountains.

Index